SHRIMPLY, INFLATION

Eiche Gardner

Kindle Direct Publishing

ISBN: 979-8-3869-0123-3

CONTENTS

YOUR MILLION DOLLAR DECISION

What would you do if you were paid one million dollars today? Would you buy a new car? Or maybe you'd pay off debt? Some might get a rush from gambling the money at a casino or in the stock market. Maybe donate it to your favorite charity? Did the option of saving the money come to mind? Having some money set aside for a rainy day isn't a bad idea.

What if you knew that one million dollars this year wouldn't be worth a million next year? Would this change your plans for the money? Almost certainly it would. If one million dollars were worth a single dollar less next year, we probably wouldn't care. However, if the million dollars were worth half as much next year, we'd want to spend it all this year. Now imagine that one million dollars will be worth two million next year. Now we won't want to part with a single dime!

Let's talk about why one million dollars today is not worth a million next year, what that means, and what the average Joe or Jane can do about it. And I'll show you fascinating and extreme real-world examples of how inflation made a million dollars one week worthless the next.

HOW INFLATION STEALS YOUR MONEY

Most people would say that money now is worth more than money in the future, because of inflation. But why? Inflation is when the prices of goods or services we buy, like food, rent, and gas, go up over time. Rising prices means that money this year will buy less next year. How much less depends on the rate of inflation. For example, a 2% annual inflation rate means that in one year prices rose by 2%.

Inflation can be caused by changes to either the supply for or demand of goods and services.

Cost-push inflation happens when there's an increase in the price of making goods or offering services. This increase in price could be caused by an increase in wages, higher raw material costs, or increased taxes. In any case, the increase in cost to the supplier is pushed onto the end consumer through higher selling prices, which we see as inflation.

You may have heard that inflation is caused by "too much money chasing too few goods." When that happens, it's called demand-pull inflation. With demand-pull inflation, high demand puts pressure on the supply chain. The increased pressure on the supply chain leads to suppliers passing increased costs onto consumers, which again you see as inflation.

Let's briefly discuss "deflation." Think of deflation as the opposite of inflation, or what happens when the inflation rate is negative. Deflation means that the purchasing power of money increases over time. Deflation can occur due to a decrease in demand for goods and services, or an increase in the supply of goods and services while the supply of money stays the same.

Famed economist Ludwig von Mises gave a lecture in 1958 about the nature of inflation. He discussed the common misconception that government money printing causes inflation. It's true that this can ultimately lead to inflation, but not for the reasons you may think. As Ludwig explains, imagine a government printing money but not spending it. Prices won't change in the broader economy until this money enters circulation; therefore, it's not the act of printing money that drives inflation, but, rather, the additional currency entering the economy that does.

Another common misconception that Ludwig addresses is the notion that increased government spending causes inflation. It doesn't. Simplifying Ludwig's explanation, imagine that the government needs to fund construction of an expensive new bridge. The government chooses to get the money to construct the bridge through taxation. In the economy, every dollar that the government puts toward building the bridge is a dollar that citizens who were taxed do not have to spend themselves. In this case, the same amount of money is chasing the same number of goods, thus no inflation.

Assume now that instead of paying for the expensive new bridge through taxation the government decides to print money to pay for it because raising taxes is unpopular with voters. In this case, every dollar that the government uses for the project is fresh into the economy. Compared to the case using tax dollars, there's more money chasing the same number of goods. Government spending can cause inflation, but it depends on the source of the money.

Ludwig had some interesting comments about the gold standard and how its end exacerbated inflation. The gold standard is when a country's government or central bank promises to exchange an amount of its currency for a promised amount of gold. Pegging the value of the currency to a precious metal helps to stabilize its value, but this won't halt inflation entirely and it limits money printing, since the government must have enough gold to fulfill the promise of the gold standard. The US broke from the gold standard in 1971.

Ludwig says that inflation is a government policy— in other words, a deliberate choice.

With the end of the gold standard, the promise that every dollar was backed by a fixed amount of gold vanished with it. Governments intentionally moved away from the gold standard to an "inflationary system." While a return to the gold standard in the United States is unrealistic, the system had the benefit of forcing governments to raise taxes to fund projects or programs. Ludwig suggests that the inflationary system gives people the perspective that the government has limitless means at its disposal. Like the bridge project example above, governments printing money to finance themselves leads to more money in the economy chasing the same number of goods, and thus, inflation. The illusion of the government having limitless means by printing money is essentially just the government pulling value from existing currency. Governments don't have bottomless pockets.

Since inflation is a policy, what are the levers governments can pull to control it? One lever is monetary policy. The gold standard is an example of monetary policy.

Since mid 2022 through the start of 2023, the Federal Reserve has been raising interest rates to fight inflation. But what does this mean? The Federal Reserve, or "the Fed," is the central bank of the United States. It was created in 1913 to provide a stable and flexible monetary and financial system. The Fed's responsibilities include regulating banks, conducting monetary policy, and promoting financial stability. When you hear about the Fed "raising interest rates," this means that they are adjusting the federal funds rate. The federal funds rate is the interest rate at which banks lend money to and borrow from each other. A change in the federal funds rate impacts borrowing and lending rates for businesses and consumers like you. For instance, raising the federal funds rate makes borrowing money more expensive, which encourages everyone to save money. This draws money out of the economy, which in turn lowers inflation. The Fed targets an annual inflation rate of 2%.

PROTECT YOURSELF
FROM INFLATION

Is inflation a good or bad thing? And what can I do about it? Now that we know what inflation is, we can tackle these questions.

Inflation can be seen as a good and a bad thing. Generally, a moderate level of inflation is considered healthy for an economy. It indicates that the economy is growing, and there's demand for goods and services. However, high levels of inflation are harmful, leading to economic instability and making it difficult for consumers and businesses to plan.

A little bit of inflation encourages spending and investment. When prices are rising, consumers are likely to make purchases sooner rather than later to avoid paying higher prices in the future. Businesses are more inclined to invest in new projects and expand their operations if they believe that demand for goods and services will continue to grow.

On the other hand, when prices are rising too quickly it's challenging, if not impossible, for consumers and businesses to plan. It reduces the purchasing power of savings and fixed-income investments, such as bonds and pensions. This can be particularly harmful for retirees and those on fixed incomes, who struggle to keep up with rising prices.

In addition, high enough inflation leads to a more rapid decrease in the value of a country's currency than would be expected, as investors begin to lose confidence in the currency's ability to hold its value. This can lead to a decrease in international trade and investment, further damaging the economy.

You cannot escape inflation, but you can mitigate it.

Investing in precious metals and properties is a common strategy that's considered a hedge against, or protection from, inflation. The idea is that the value of gold, property, and other assets are independent of paper currency. Over the long term, the price of these assets rises because their inherent value is fixed. There's a risk here, of course. There's no guarantee that these assets will sell for a fair price.

Stocks, bonds, and retirement funds can grow in value over time, and this growth can outpace inflation. Some assets are riskier than others, and there's no guarantee that investment growth will outpace inflation. There's also the potential to lose some or all your investments.

Some assets are specifically inflation-protected, like United States I bonds. The US government offers treasury savings bonds backed by the full faith and credit of the US Treasury. Many view this as a "risk-free" investment since losing your investment would require the United States to default or to refuse to or be unable to pay back its loans. I bonds started being offered in 1998. They have a composite interest rate comprised of two separate rates: a fixed rate determined at date of purchase, and an inflation-adjusted rate that updates every six months to make sure your investment at least keeps pace with inflation.

There are some limitations though. There's an annual limit of $10,000 electronic and $5,000 paper I bonds per person, per year. I bonds are not marketable—meaning, you can't sell or transfer them, and you cannot cash the bond until a year from the purchase date. Additionally, if you're a US citizen, any interest earned on the bond, including from the inflation adjusted rate, is taxed by the federal government at the bond's maturity or when the bond is cashed. The tax can be waived if the interest is used to pay for qualifying educational expenses.

Lastly, inflation is beneficial to those in fixed-rate debt if the inflation rate outpaces the interest rate of that debt. When you borrow money, you pay back that money and then some. The extra bit you pay back over time is called interest, and it's how lenders make their money. While the amount you're expected to pay back might be fixed, your wages rise with inflation. When the inflation rate is higher than the interest rate of the debt, you're effectively paying back the same amount but with more money in your pocket.

Be wary of deflation! While money being worth more is nice, owing more money isn't. This is what happens when you have debt with deflation—debtholders owe more because the value of their debt increases. Don't worry about this too much though. Since deflation isn't so great for large and powerful debtholders, such as banks and governments, it's viewed as a bad thing, and typically monetary policy seeks to avoid deflation.

THE ULTIMATE ECONOMIC CATASTROPHE— HYPERINFLATION

Hyperinflation is inflation to the extreme. It's a situation where the prices of goods and services increase rapidly, leading to a rapid decrease in the value of money. There is no cutoff for when inflation becomes hyperinflation. But, as opposed to inflation which happens noticeably on the scale of decades or years, hyperinflation happens noticeably on the scale of weeks or days. Let's explore the consequences of hyperinflation by looking at some examples from history.

Hyperinflation happened in France in the 1790s during the French Revolution.

The primary cause was the excessive printing of paper money known as assignats, which were issued by the revolutionary government to finance its war efforts and to pay off its debts. The government began printing assignats at an unrestricted rate. As the money supply grew, the value of the currency began to decline. This led to an increase in the prices of goods and services, which, in turn, led to a further increase in the money supply, as the government printed more money to meet the rising costs. This created a vicious cycle of inflation, which led to hyperinflation.

The value of the assignats declined rapidly, and within a year, the currency lost over 97% of its value. The hyperinflation caused widespread social and economic unrest, with many people unable to afford necessities like food and clothing. The economy was paralyzed as businesses closed, and many people lost their jobs.

The insightful book *Fiat Money Inflation in France* by Andrew Dickson White discusses some interesting measures that the revolutionary government took to tame inflation. It tried implementing price controls and introducing new currencies. This didn't fix inflation. Then, the government outlawed using foreign currency and precious metals to force people to use the national currency. At one point not using the national currency in an exchange for goods carried the death penalty. Stranger yet, later even discussing not using the national currency in an exchange for goods also carried the death penalty. Ultimately, all of these measures proved ineffective, and the government was forced to default on its debts. A new government took over and eventually stabilized the economy by moving away from paper currency.

Hyperinflation in France during the French Revolution serves as a reminder of the dangers posed by excessive money printing to cover government costs, and the importance of sound economic policies to maintaining economic stability.

Okay, history is fascinating, but hyperinflation couldn't possibly happen in the modern world— could it?

Hyperinflation happened as recently as the 2000s in Zimbabwe.

The hyperinflation between the late 1990s and early 2000s in Zimbabwe is considered one of the worst cases of hyperinflation in history. The root cause of the crisis was a combination of poor economic policies, political instability, and corruption.

The government of Zimbabwe started printing

money to finance their expenses, such as farm seizures, social programs, and the war in Congo, leading to a significant increase in the money supply. However, the economy was not producing enough goods and services to match this increase, which led to excess demand and inflation.

As inflation began rising, the government imposed price controls. This made things worse. Retailers were unable to cover their costs, leading to shortages and black markets. The government responded by printing more money to pay for imports, leading to a further increase in inflation.

At its peak, annual inflation in Zimbabwe was estimated to be over 79 billion percent in November 2008. Prices of goods and services doubled every 24 hours, making it impossible for people to afford food, medicine, and housing. Many businesses closed, and unemployment rose significantly.

The hyperinflation also had political consequences because it eroded public trust in the government and led to social unrest. People lost faith in the national currency, and many resorted to using foreign currencies like the US dollar and South African rand.

When Money Destroys Nations by Philip Haslam and Russell Lamberti discusses the role of fuel coupons in the Zimbabwean economy during hyperinflation. The government tried to force people to use its currency by making bartering using foreign currencies and precious metals illegal. People turned to fuel. Fuel provides power, doesn't degrade over time, is used for maintaining infrastructure, and drives the overall economy. Because of fuel's critical role in the economy, the government couldn't restrict the bartering of it like it could foreign currency or precious metals without risking total economic collapse.

Fuel was so important that fuel companies were given special permission by the Zimbabwean government to trade in foreign currencies. Fuel companies began accepting foreign currency in exchange for fuel coupons. Zimbabweans could redeem the coupons for fuel. The fuel companies would then use the foreign currency earned from the sale of coupons to purchase fuel from nearby countries to exchange for coupons within Zimbabwe.

As you can imagine, fuel coupons quickly became a new, alternate currency in Zimbabwe. This made fuel companies effectively into banks, where people could deposit foreign currency for fuel coupons, analogous to paper money pegged to the value of fuel. However, the fuel companies began to issue more fuel coupons than there was fuel that the coupons could be exchanged for. This is like how banks lend more money than they can pay back. Remember demand-pull inflation we discussed earlier in this book? As we've said repeatedly, it's inflation driven by too much money chasing too few goods. Well, it turns out that principle can apply to anything being used as currency, even fuel coupons. Before long, amidst the hyperinflation of the Zimbabwean national currency there was also hyperinflation in the value of Zimbabwean fuel coupons.

Ultimately, to combat hyperinflation, in 2009 the government introduced the Zimbabwean dollar. The new currency was pegged to the US dollar, and price controls were lifted. The government also stopped printing money and implemented fiscal reforms. These measures helped to stabilize the economy and began pulling the country out of hyperinflation.

Hyperinflation is an economic catastrophe that self-perpetuates and takes significant time to recover from. As the examples of the French Revolution and the Zimbabwean economic collapse illustrate, hyperinflation can cause massive social and economic instability alongside economic and political distrust. The best way for an indivudual to fight hyperinflation is to move themselves and their family some place else with a stable economy.

KEY TAKEAWAYS

Inflation is when the value of money decreases over time. It happens when the supply of goods or services is disrupted or when there's too much money chasing too few goods or services. The inflationary system in the United States is managed by the Fed through monetary policy. The Fed targets an annual inflation rate of 2%.

Inflation can be good or bad depending on how large the rate of inflation is and how long it lasts. It's best when inflation is small and predictable, keeping the economy stimulated and providing a level of stability that allows everyone to plan financially year-to-year. It's a bad thing when the inflation rate is high and unpredictable since investments become discouraged by financial uncertainty and savings erode quickly. Some ways for the average person to fight inflation include investing in physical assets that are less impacted by inflation like precious metals, or investing in financial assets which grow and break even with or outpace inflation.

Hyperinflation is self-sustaining and kills a country's economy. France's revolutionary government was powerless to halt hyperinflation through use of the guillotine in the 1790s. And in Zimbabwe in the 2000s, hyperinflation was so prevalent that it even affected the value of fuel coupons which began replacing the country's worthless currency. The risk of hyperinflation has not vanished in the modern world. And if it comes knocking, the best answer is to move away.